IN

NATURAL

LIGHT

MICHAEL
ANANIA

IN
NATURAL
LIGHT

ASPHODEL PRESS
Wakefield, Rhode Island
& London

Published by Asphodel Press

Grateful acknowledgment is made to the following periodicals in which some of these poems first appeared: *Álora, La Bien Cercada* (Má laga), *Chicago Review, Columbia Review of the Arts, Frank, Indelible Ink, LVNG, Notre Dame Review, Poetry East, Rio, Tri-Quarterly* and *Zamisdat*. CD recorded at the studios of WFMT-FM (Chicago).

Music on CD: "Let the Rest of the World Go By" by Guy Lombardo, and pieces from Clavierübung II, by J.S. Bach, interpreted by Gustav Leonhardt.

Cover art: "Diner with Red Door" by Ralph Goings, courtesy of O.K. Harris Works of Art, New York, NY.

LIBRARY OF CONGRESS
CATALOGING-IN-PUBLICATION DATA

Anania, Michael, 1939–
    In natural light / by Michael Anania.
       p.   cm.
    ISBN 1–55921–270–5 (alk. paper)
    I. Title.
PS3551.N25I49   1999
811'.54 — dc21   98–33656
                                 CIP

CONTENTS

For Anthony and Andrew

"Physical transparency can not explain perceptual transparency."

Fabio Matelli

"though brilliance in the air lingers"

Thomas McGrath

I

"A Place That's Known"

Out on the front step fifty years ago,
my mother beside the four o'clocks
smoking her last Chesterfield of the night,
locusts strumming, radio dramas and anger
practiced through open windows, the Plaza
beginning just where her anklets crossed,
American elms opening a span of western sky.

Sky outside her hospital window
spring-gray and full of the plains, droplets
sigh against the glass: wind out of Norfolk
and Kearney, brimming their emptiness.
We are silent now watching the thin,
transparent oxygen tube rise and fall
at the vein where it crosses her neck.

One and one and one, not a sequence
but something failing to start, ending.
Her hands seem longer than I had thought,
the still curve from wrist bone to fingertip,
fingernail ridges the same as my own;

3

my hand, my fingers begin and end in hers.
Slipping away, they say, one breath, no others.

I remember singing, a dance spun
across the linoleum's worn flowers,
her hair pressed into his chest, the Zenith's
pale dial, words of the song that stopped
the dancing, everyone staring into
the music, Seven-up blushed with port, war:
"I'd like to leave it all behind and go and find . . ."

somewhere in the West, in a space of green
edged with gold and sky blue, something the Plaza
might have given way to if we listened hard and held tight,
like the night his face appeared at the back window,
hitchhiked from Kearney, rail thin and cold,
and she sighed and scolded and leaned against him.
"What hospital?" he said, wishing it away.

That night we huddled into our wishes,
as later into relics and stories, evenings
full of the past, the green strong box opened,
bits of his life and hers spread out over

white chenille, each object held and named:
rosary, scapular, catechism, gun,
rewrapped in cloth or paper and locked away.

"Your father," "your grandmother," "my dad"
she said into the broken night, sirens edging
toward us, the fight across the way spilt
down the steps onto to the Plaza's hopscotch,
knife flash or skillet lid, a razor's band
of blue darkness moving across soft skin
as smoothly as sweat, blood quick as a tear.

Summer night, poverty's continual rage,
voices, hands, fists rising and falling
accusations and recriminations
breaking through windows, out of doors.
"Your father," she said, "your grandmother,"
the boat, the island, the train, the long dusty
tilt of the world, how they sang and danced.

One voice, all those years, against the clamor,
stories and names against blood-soaked hand towels,
against heels pounding down the walk, screams,

drowned children, scaldings, flesh drawn up and pink,
stretcher after stretcher, "cover their eyes,"
their faces, so many stomachs clutched in pain.
"Your father," she said, "my mother" and "sleep."

December Commonplace

Bare foxglove stems
and remnant cosmos
sketched across this

morning's snowfall,
sunlight fissured
among seed crowns;

we are tilting past
solstice; dead plant
shadows, like blue

veins in pale skin,
branch through crystals
and course and grow.

Eclogue

How sudden they seem,
the gradual lives
of flowers, or the faces
you see in the brief
light of a "B" stop
taking, as you always
do, the "A" train.

October Evening

for Pat Nelson

West of the near west side,
beyond the ragged line of
watertowers and chimneys

and the tufted nylon rose
upholstery city sunset,
the day is making its way

with you into the past,
a slant of clear light
among darkening branches

or the Cascades' evening sheen
the glacier cups into
a thousand years of snow.

Apples

for Robert Creeley

The news—precious little
to hold onto—cuts and burns.
In Buffalo, six taxi drivers,
murdered, their hearts
cut out and carried away.
Lebanese shards. All across
the country victims sprawl.
Terrorists in New York.

In Indiana, just south of the dunes,
brown cider is put out in Dixie cups,
apples cinched up in plastic bags
along the floor—Jonathans, Red
and Golden Delicious, Winesaps,
frost-skinned Cortlands, Romes—
shelves of amber, home-strained
honey, prize-winning gourds.

At the edge of his new blacktop
parking lot, Anderson, the owner,

tries to explain the two turkeys
in his yard to three Vietnamese
loading apples into a blue Chevrolet.
The tom fans his tail and struts
along the bellying wire fence.
"Look, look," he says, waving.

Winesap as though responding,
topple and roll every which way.
The Vietnamese smile and nod,
pointing at what Anderson
and his turkey have just done—
autumn and gravity, apples
unevenly spinning, feathers
flurried above bright asphalt.

"America," he says, "America,"
as though this were their chance
to see it all at once, part question,
part exclamation, an explanation
insisted upon in the moment,
then lost, his hands at his sides.

They are nodding, *yes, yes,* palms pressed
together, the scattered apples at rest.

Perhaps, it is always true that each
occasion is its own center, that in
its moment the wobbling Winesap's stem
is the axis to our irregular pasts,
motions that curve inward as they fall
across contending radians, waves
of news and weather invisibly
symmetrical and lost among the leaves.

Somewhat Gray and Graceful

for Reginald Shepherd

Left behind. Consider the frayed
horizon and the likelihood
of birds. Someone in a photograph
glances upward and flight

extrapolates itself as a story
proposed by one thing and then
another, each surface accomplished,
each act a definition, the self

in a prospect of birds, flight
arrived at in the unconsidered
assumption of flight, finches
sprung forward and eased against

the edge of sight, the improbable
reach of this and that, somewhat gray
and graceful, doves in their white rush
like breath anticipating speech.

From the Petrarchan Folio (42r)

I.

In the hand of the original scribe,
an inverted triangle— it says,
she had been seen in Avignon,
her face, at least, in Simone Martini's
wall, long since destroyed.

So they presumed upon her,
each one of them scribbling:
Bembo in 1472; Segni in his own
sonnet, where she is said to
triumph, though he set down
his own name in an acrostic,
Laureo, then, and Laurentio
joined at the poem's first corner.

II.

Laureo, quick among the leaves,
all that is said of her, years even

past her death, the pen's stiff
whispering at the point of her
initial; then, touch, the scribe's
stained fingers, stain of all that
might be said in her name, name
initiating this rustling, tree just past
his window asway with her.
Laureo, spoken, Laurentio, proposed;
her self fleshed, as the penpoint
sighs or the eye catches her initial
letter and the tongue lifts itself
to the voiceless onset of her name.

As Semblance, Though

"non siamo . . . non vogliamo"
Montale

The nothing—or the not—supposes, of course,
and gestures into some certain absence.
You thought as much, might have said so quickly,

in passing; distinctly absolute, furtive
and improbable, this tentative void,
quiet now, and the jet engines roar skyward,

the refrigerator hums, then shudders still,
lights in the hallway, shadows at the door;
imagine storefronts and littered gangways,

someone slouched darkly at the corner,
a mote in your eye, perhaps, nothing
worth noting; nonetheless, a hand moving,

the jitter of skin over skin and now a taste
of copper, like pennies in your mouth,
the air in its own time adjusted to your face.

You are the shape it takes of nothing,
a border urged outward, speaking its own
incessant edge, as water breaks and curls,

river scrawl meandering, naming the catch
in your throat, all that lies beyond whatever
seems defensible, ridge or hill, profiled

revetments, sighs, sightlines among shallows,
reeds and cattails. Nothing, of course.
The absolutist stomp begun again; lift me

homeward, you might have said to the wind—
or into, or against—its vortices curling
their smoke trailed petals across your face.

More than zero, always, and more than one,
the self and its selves edging along successive
thresholds, sill after sill, a blue contentment

as certain as the sky, washed over hillside
and treeline and all those distances it recedes
from as the land slips past you or the river

flexes beneath its own shimmering skin,
each instance of light play and water
silted to the next, each hued with its own past.

Unaccountable, the swirl of occasions—
sparrows churn street dusts; catfish and carp
furl their way through their own suspended lands,

each present gulped in, then pushed away, fins
working past against past, some earlier
shore unsettled here, sun struck and tempered.

The "devil's fingers" clutched into wet silt,
lengths of stone, fused, they said, by ground strikes
of branch lightning, the river's leeched current snagged;

"devil's finger"—because dark and crooked
or pointing earthward, full of sullen portent
or possessive, hooking the river like loose cloth,

though they are mostly not quartz but calcium,
the cuttle-bones of giant squid, tentacles, beaks
and ink drawn off into the soil, river

only briefly stained, time counted out in longer
intervals than intent has patience for; tree
lilt, silt swirl, the earth's long hush humming.

II

"And This Is Free"

for Sterling Plumpp

In this film, now thirty years old,
a blues band is playing on Maxwell Street,
a woman with narrow legs and white shoes
dances beneath her own raised hands;

at the curb a man extends three fingers
toward the music, feeling its edge spill
toward him as though it were a subtle
property of the air, a Braille he reads

there, sentence by sentence, his smile
tilting away, his balance uncertain;
ecstatic, he nods, yes, that's right,
sorrow's joy now trembling in his grasp.

Two girls lean against a stained wall
in unison; arms, legs, shopping bags pass;
fingers bend into fret-lines, fingernails
along the shoaling strings flash like wavetips,

and the song says, "You spent all my money
on whiskey and wine," Meister Brau boxes
filled with broken-faced dolls, the stitched
creases where their arms fold forward darkening,

and the song says, "Love aint half as good
as you said it would be," a tu-tone jacket
flapping at his sides, another dancer
spins once and talks back to the guitar;

brown paper twisted up tight, bottle cap
turned down against it; pass it around,
it is a breath that catches in your breath
something going from hand to hand, its words

thick and burning in your throat, and the song says,
"Left me" and "alone" and "like a river"
and "jelly roll" and the street has a wet sheen,
"fly away, fly away" and the song says,

sunstreaked window and security grate,
doorway, doorway, a forearm of gold watches,

shadows draped like damp cloth, rooflines and hubcaps,
and the song says, "like a sweet girl should,"

city curling its long arms inward, "string
of pearls, string of pearls," lost in the beat of it,
hands (always), lined palms offering diamonds
sideways like secret insinuations;

a boy on his knees in the street hand jiving
a cardboard box, a woman selling housewares
reaches toward him—she wants her box back;
pennies skip over paving bricks, and the song says,

"out in the kitchen with a butcher knife,"
an edge to whatever moves through shadow
and out into the street's mid-Sunday light,
fingering the chord into place, voice leaning,

amps set up among cinders and broken glass,
hat pushed forward, meaning *free-and-easy*,
and the song says, "raise my hand . . . feel better"
and "if only you just understand."

The market goes on, bundles of socks,
tee shirts, coats, jackets, boxes of records
in tattered paper sleeves, pencils, crayons,
roll-ends of linoleum, window shades,

cards of bobby pins and bluebird barrettes,
rubber-banded place-settings, paper cups,
dollar bills fanned from raised fists, snap counts,
fingers popping, change chanted thumb to palm.

And the song says "you," meaning *he* or *she*,
and "me," meaning *you and I*, and "my,"
meaning *ours*, and "so good," meaning *so good,*
then "I guess I got a touch of the blues."

Some Other Spring

after Teddy Wilson

"You know how it goes,"
    he said—the quick shift
        of light and dark, the day

itself like music,
    playing, an instance
        of balance, presumed,

like the moment,
    entirely imagined,
        then seen, when the ball

hesitates, spinning, against
    blue sky, bright day, its
        first green drawn along

dark branches, the arc
    of so much to account
        for in time, time in his

27

left hand's intermittent
certainties, the right
airborne, at play, playing.

Things Aint What They Used To Be

for Peter and Marilyn

heel and toe
    Capezios
        skirt unfurled
and spinning
    lights asway
        Les Elgart
fingers
    locked into
        moist fingers

Sequence Composed on Gray Paper

for David Mahler

i.

mid-January mums
and white statice,
the nightlong hum
of things, wind
in the doorsill,
the furnace sighing

ii.

at the curved line
wind hones along
the snow's extended
leeward edge, the sound
of a glass bottle
spun on smooth stone

iii.

past the expressway,
roofline after roofline,
the evening reddening,

chimney and stand-pipe
smoke like pinfeathers;
saltlines along the highway's
balustrade echoing

iv.

warm breath on cold fingers,
cloud cupped there, voiceless,
between thought and sound

v.

across the evening river—
gleam of the Burlington
tracks, the bright windows
of Ruby's Cleaners; someone
an Oriental woman, I think,
is running down a narrow
aisle of clothing, Ruby,
perhaps, turning sharply
to the left and out of sight,
an instant of urgency,
suits and dresses rippling

vi.

Wednesday morning in the Loop,
thighs quick against thighs,
traffic and slush playing along

vii.

south of Roosevelt on Canal,
this winter's imperative
scrawled cursive in the road
scrum gurried to an eighteen-
wheeler: "Vamp to Chorus!"

Out & About

after Marvin Bell

A whale of a good time he had, all things considered; the
    folks at the company outing more or less contented,
    as well, ambled back to cars and mini-vans pulled up
    against creosoted parking barriers, the smoke from
    UNISYS Breakfast in the Pines sausages and griddle
    cakes hovering above Park District barbeques;
"hmm," he thought as radial tires bit into crushed
    limestone and small-talk sped toward an impending
    quiet like water swirling at the drain;
some things remain difficult—zippers, punctuation,
    creeping charlie, hairlines of all sorts, the small screws
    that held the side-pieces to his glasses, tenses,
but harmony, if you don't ask too much of it and spare
    yourself Germanic idealism, seems rather more likely
    than not;
considering the leaves, for example, he decided—just like
    that—to be at ease with their descent, said 'sycamore'
    under his breath and the leaves of the sycamore fell,
    not at his urging exactly but with his accord, likewise
    alder and copper beech,

so language, his language, if not language in general,
  seemed efficacious;
"morning," he'd say to whoever he passed, kicking his way
  through the leafy path, and some—not all, of
  course—would say "morning" in return,
and if he had a hat on, he would tip it, an act of such
  simple pleasure that he took to wearing a hat of some
  sort every morning,
choosing from a box in the hall closet fedoras, pork pies,
  denim brakeman's caps, a white painter's cap with the
  world half-covered in paint on the crown, a straw
  Stetson chewed at the edges, a replica vintage Dodger
  cap he thought of as sized to a replica Duke Snyder,
  a wheat-colored boater, deer-stalkers, brooding
  Borsalinos,
each one selected by some undetermined principle he
  invented for the moment of choice, never, as a kind
  of rule, second guessing himself;
"morning," he'd say to friend and foe alike, in a flat even
  tone of voice, neither assertion nor question but a
  gesture of assent which could with little trouble
  become mutual,
or "afternoon" or "evening" depending on the time of day,

obviously, but "morning"—he preferred "morning" as
	a greeting, so preferred strolling in the morning,
and the faces around him were interchangeable like the
	parking meters he passed, each moving at the same
	pace toward separate but identical catastrophes;
he considered the woman coming out of the meadow, a
	kleenex wrapped around her finger, dabbing at a spot
	of maple syrup on her blouse, then moistening the
	tip of the kleenex with her tongue and dabbing
	again, each time, he supposed, tasting the syrup's
	cloying sweetness, and in sequence, each taste would
	be less strong and the mark on the cloth above her
	left breast less dark, though neither would, even if
	she never reached her Plymouth Voyager but walked
	and dabbed on and on, ever vanish entirely;
"o maple tree," he said out loud, "the sweet stain of
	things, here in time's flattening curve, the hyperbola's
	apparent, twin infinities, love's old sweet song, a
	proposed axis between us."

Bell Sounds

for Ralph Mills (after Jaccottet)

Angled in, crevacing
the edged places where
darkness shapes itself;

imagine all those
centuries of sea
water, star-swept

rocktips and slow time.
Is it shale at long
last, sediments layered

with weather systems,
one after another?
The inlet's double

reel of foams crossing
foams. Cloudprint. Not
an image but consequence,

what the sentence
predicted or happened upon,
the way things turn,

then turn back again,
shoals in the self—stone-
work's uneven coils

in the ear's own shell. Rain
shadow across stone, each darkness
layering another, as sound

crests over sound. What-
ever moves here is nothing
wind and water have not made.

As Though

for Elaine Galen

as though the pine sap
smudged into your fingertips
mattered, you scrub at it;

blue spruce branches piled
at the culvert, bright November
air, yellow strains of maple

along the drive; things
begin, endings, for example,
like sleep, one thought

and then another, darkness
chilling your arm, memory—
and in a slow instant,

like a radio switched off,
still playing—what is
remembered as forgetfulness

Missing Matter

Of course, it is improbable
that in all of this endless turning
things do not simply fly apart;
stars uncluster, your hand gesturing
just now, or mine, grow vague and disperse
like wings in sunlight, more light than wing,
or galaxies, more darkness than light.

Knowledge has grown so wistful, as though
the gathering weight of fact makes fact
improbable, numbers crunching numbers
until they break and scatter like twigs
underfoot, brittle suppositions,
nothing you can be expected to
account for, someone else's question,

the day's accumulation of objects
turned out into the impending night
like dust and lint swept across a door sill,
the door, backing into the evening's shadows,
itself a proposition. Hold on, fast, back,

your eyes pressed open by the sheer rush of things,
though nothing past this threshold is defined.

Strands of sense, course the music takes,
blues chord caught in your fingers—*so long, so long*—
had hoped the prairie or the river or the neon sign,
time like tendrils, a grammar's fingered pages,
the highway spun like hope out of the self's ceaseless
hunger—*Sweet Jesus, Sweet Jesus*—that part of need
so certain it ripples like water across blank spaces.

Songs Intended for Familiar Places

i.

light along an edge
    —say what you will!—
        the surface diminished,

color suddenly gone
    or its absence noted,
        all of a sudden, like

a snapshot held up
    against a scene it
        only partially depicts

ii.

slipped into a line
    of trees, evening
        voices wade in privet

shallows, footfalls
    imagined as they fall;
        this nocturne supposes

nightbugs and traffic,
    the residual hum of sodium
        arc lights, their yellow

haze imposed across
    the presumed nightlong
        rotation of the stars

iii.

street not so much
    a bordered plane as
        an enclosure of walls

asphalt and streetlights
    asway with arms, shoulders,
        hand pressed into moist

hand or blade-quick,
    something clutched fast,
        the ready anger of it

iv.

downward, leaf after leaf,
   grit embossed into the heels
     of your hands, the self's

lines and ridges scored
   with loosened aggregate
     and burning, sky of deep

periwinkle, birds like
   check marks angled into
     bright, smoke-trailed clouds

v. (duet)

slow march, key'd cornet
   glides and mad-sweet pangs,
     all civil charms and spells;

dull rumble and the town,
   like dreams, dissolves; is it
     the sway of self that shakes

the wall? housetop beneath,
   the stars hushed and music
      doubling along the night's

slurred margins; we walk
   the dark's bright crevices,
      heel strike after heel strike

certain as anything, say
   it is here names and their
      implicit voices matter

Incidental Music

for A.K. Ramanujan, 1929-1994

i.

stylus bobbing
above dark vinyl
like a dragonfly,

Mozart, then Horace Silver,
their bright waters,
onyx spun across shale;

it must have been
the basement
used record store

on Hyde Park Blvd,
hubcaps and wheel-lugs
at eye-level; cities

seem so purposeful,
their musics half-formed,
urgent as traffic;

lake effect snow—
the day not quite cold
enough—brightens

the pavement only
momentarily, laughter
and exhaust plumes,

their sudden clarities
passing; across the Midway
science and industry twang

ii.

what flowers should we
drift along this course
of dampened asphalt

in your memory, Raman?
mullai, kurñci, maratum,
neytal, each blossom

a precinct in song:
forest, mountain,
clear stream or dark sea?

and what transpires there,
a bird among the millet,
peppervine and palmyra,

their moistened palms
extended, fresh blossoms
and finger cymbals?

in archaic Tamil, then,
"what he said," "what she said,"
generations of poets masked

along the stations of song;
nearby the city's improbable
flock of brooding parakeets

stirs a sudden iridescence
above bare box elder
and salt-nettled pines

iii.

the faith we have
in song exceeds its
melodies, notes struck

in speech we only
imagine speaking;
music surged then

hand raised in breath,
stylus fingered above
syllables; not feeling

merely, but how we take
its measure, pronounce,
inadequately, *patai,*

the fifth region, flowerless,
a place of separation, note
held against emptiness,

a saxophone sighs, steel
brush on brass, the beat
extended, *patai patai*

petals opening iridescent
birdflowers city singers
are blowing in their hands

III

As Ever

"par la lumière naturelle"

I.

in or among
  the gray unsettling
    consequence of things—

"did you sigh
  just then or simply move
    your arm across fresh linen?"

splash of pigment,
  chrome yellow, surely
    accidental, though so

much of our sense
  of things will ultimately
    depend upon it, we will

certainly suppose
  varying degrees of
    intention—"you think

you could maybe
  let me see inside,
    just once"—that is,

if one thing depicts,
  then any other thing
    might just as well, burnt

sienna or carmine red,
  ultra-marine blue, as certain
    a source as anyone might imagine;

quicksilver trails,
  the crystal fray that marks
    invisible passages; quick! quick!

a lantern among bon fires,
  flake white moths threading
    nervous light, powdery paradiso;

"I mean, as long as we're
  here amid the locust trees"
    and the shadows are all falling

in the same general
   direction, there must be
      a tune that contains this,

a box step we can count
   our way through together,
      something to catch the instant

and turn it back our way,
   feints of cursive red neon
      across wet pavement, the hum-

drum inevitability
   of truck tires, uneven
      carbon residues across concrete

II.

"uncertain of all,"
   the lapsed time so finely
      calibrated that even the shaky

false leaves opening,
   unsheathed translucent
      stem snaking toward the light,

have numbers they play at,
  and confirm, bits of soil
    tumbling slowly backward;

day by day, conformation,
  things, that is, becoming
    themselves; "how is it color

seems to matter," qualities
  that eventually adhere,
    masses of leaves and summer

darkly weighing; she said,
  as others had certainly,
    "reckoning with consequences,"

meaning the processes of
  reasoning, or was it the mind
    at play, flowers trembling

against their buds,
  liquid now, now solid,
    the simplest of equations

unformed and brushed
  across some waiting green;
    the bristles' chance impressions

in fresh paint catch
  the afternoon light,
    petal on petal petalling;

imagine, that is, the rose,
  its string of re-animated
    photographs played in among

a desire for roses,
  torqued upward into
    the descending intention

of color, however casually
  chosen, and what is said
    in time is always temporal,

hence song and dance
  swaying from axis to axis,
    words like gauds spun and spinning

After a Drawing on Papyrus

for Reg Gibbons

dark lady in the pale
fox's dream, fox
the underside
of her candor;

imagine! she says,
my will in your eyes,
your quick purpose
the onset of desire,

how the night softens
into small gestures,
scents, a moist trail,
prey as certain as

my name, now half
forgotten; O self, self,
I am drifting toward
a purer form of hunger

Edvard Munch

(Hamburg, 1995)

They gather into their own secrets,
those others, turned out of the self,
drifting as torsos among the trees.

A summer night, girls by the sea,
how she bleeds her hair across his face,
and reddening, as well, her gown

opens like a curtain to his gaze.
What have you made of these waters,
a pale column between the sun

and its reflection? Listen, listen,
they are stirring like oars in bright
wavelets, colors past all bordering,

moon and sun, dryads loosed
from their dreams. The waves rise
like hillocks, year by year, adrift

in arm, hair and pelvis, her lidded
eyes, that complex you conceived in her
aswirl in whatever she might have imagined.

Psyche and Eros

after Canova

His sepal wings and her arms petalled
upward, kiss in stamen, an absence
of pollen in stone. Is it sleep

or daydream, pause or an amplification
of the moment, kiss, an occasion

in stone, this reverie ascending
or dream hovering into the flower's

arms lifting? "Sweet Psyche," he whispers,
stone to stone as clear water (from
lip to lip, then stone to stone). "Ah Eros."

What Are Islands To Me Now

for Barbara Guest

I

carved wood, bronzes, tracings ice
crystals leave on the windowpane;
coat it with parafin, then scratch
whatever you like into the wax,
the design can be quite delicate;
an acid bath—careful, the least
splash will burn your flesh away

II

away at last, the long dark slope
of the land captured in haze,
the broad sea, sluggish at first;
my heart's ablaze, she said,
something is certain to carry
us somewhere full of purpose;
don't ask me how I know these things

III

these things left out in plain sight,
their present arrangement not the least
bit reflective of some initial
intention; consider the number of people
who pass this way each day, that certain
objects are picked up and moved around
and others may be gone entirely, stolen

IV

stolen moments, it was a song they heard
long after everyone else had gone below,
patterns in the engine's throb, perhaps,
or an actual voice, low and faltering
with emotion; if it hadn't been for the song,
he said, or its possibility, the mere likelihood
of pattern and recurrence and their consequence

V

consequence, might as well say it,
an event of single consequence; imagine
the mire of occasions and our habits
of attribution, the more or less troubling
accidents of speech, collisions of all sorts;
dear rushing heart, is there less to us
or more or simply just what meets the eye

VI

the eye is now the problem, imperiums
of sight, one after another, glance, gaze
or glare; do you remember the orange itself,
some other orange, or paint curling light
into a skin of apparent brightness, incidents
of touch, not merely recollected or assumed
but edged into the space between canvas and pigment

VII

pigment of choice or chance, the night's
permanence in steel grey, oiled and polished,
the brush of chilled dampness across your cheek,
curiously reassuring, the way you sometimes
bite your lip against the possibility that nothing
occurs even at that short distance, a proposition
in which cause matters or choice or deliberation

VIII

deliberate as the trail of the immediate
past, the line of sea foam opening behind us,
its certainties loosened among wavetips;
of course, we have a sense of destination,
that a line of green trees, underscored
with white sand inevitably awaits us,
a shore against which all these moments fall

IX

falls like light across her outstretched hand,
along the shell he raises to his lips,
rustles among the brittle edges of leaves
its own busy agitations; sand castings,
the intricate weights and measures, domestic
gods and godesses, balanced against seed grain
and sea salt, briefly certain in their sight

X

sighting across her upper arm, the way
it was turned toward him and her breast
his first horizon, the room a focal haze;
a snarl of sunlight among carnations,
not so much seen as imagined in the sun's glare,
red picot cream colored petals recalled
more than seen, the moment teetering there

Oranges and Lemons

It hardly matters.
there at the easel,
brushing away at

the tangibility
of a morning's work,
the oranges and lemons

of an obsessive
still-life quickening,
the thick, pale presence

of things almost
gone, as though
this labor against

an obvious surface
is where the art began
and the fruit arranged

on the table, a mere
occasion of light through
sun-streaked tall windows.

De Kooning

NY, April 1997

How is it the light
grows furious once again,
yellow and orange,
then wafts into
a green clarity?

She waits in curve
and fold, the cleft
of her drifting
in a white rest,
a blank space
that urges space
along, the way
in music silence
drives the song.

Out of Dazzlement

for Elizabeth Streb

I.

Two notes unevenly
played as shore and sea,
the trim lyre curled across

sight lines in salt spray
sporting lapis amid foam,
sounded Okeanos

briefly held, wave after wave,
sunlit droplets struck like forge
sparks, the air ringing.

II.

All that sways in breezes now,
quick-limbed configurings
flash through froth and pine,

names each local apprehension
set in song and said to be,
a flower among the dunes,

perhaps, or bit of dolerite
in wet sand. Whatever is asserted
is played in this uncertain dance.

III.

Arms raised, she turns,
her fingers trailed in spinning,
as though her own velocity

pulled them that way; clutches
at it, catching hold of space
itself; her right foot strikes

the floor, elbows now at her
sides, fists drawn tight, pushing
at once outward and back.

IV.

Supposes the moment forms
itself around her as wavefall
forms the shore, that bright air

churns into tide pools at her feet
and darkens there, runnels speeding
away, brusque landfall, wind shoaling

against salt grasses, seabirds crying;
head turned, her palms extended as
lines of kelp scrawled across phosphors.

V.

Only motion, its play
against and among, defines—
bandaged toes to floor,

chalked hands along the air's
implicit torso, a lunge
into a dream of flight,

light's insistence just where
the wave is lifted and breaks
along the salt edge of song.

Study with Several Figures,
Incompletely Recalled

In the curious vase painting, Denise Martin;
with a certain individuality of drawing, Joyce Sales;
possibly here as at Athens, Archie Brown;
of the actual ceremony, proudly, Jack Corbin.
He took a sparrow in his hand and covered it.

Barbara Cook charmingly set forth, clearly traceable;
propitiations and appeasements, the saving grace,
as with Judy Donahue or Larry Oswald;
one is drawing water from the wall basin,
Lonzo Patterson; nothing could be clearer.

The scene takes the form of a simple procession.
So, in early days, the more prominent Pat Olson;
Joe Richards, Tom Marsh and Stanley Stinnette,
Charles Urwin and Gail Stephens—images
and puppets thrown from the bridge, sharply sundered.

There was an element of mystery, more and more
human and kindly, objects or beings, if we prefer.

Assuredly no one, without the inscriptions, would
have ventured to conjecture the inscribed names.
Elaine Slama and Charlene Nitz blameless as to

the trust invested in them, fair born or fair birth;
from fire, sun and serpent, Dale Joons; couched
in language, actually existing, Joyce Hollins;
here they stand in sharp contrast, Jim Helm,
Ruth Kirby, Dina Ingram, Wesley Henry,

perhaps over-inspired, at or near Argos.
The reason is not clear but the fact is well established.
Sarah Harris smites her timbrel in token; Tom Hopkins
will be in part determined later; Doris Fricke
spread southward, red-figured; Mickey Ogden,

Darrell Nutter, Carolyn Otto, Viola Buffington
finely conceived, deduced from the relief in question.
Art has left us no certain representation.
The style is late and florid, as though they were
almost the exclusive property of the stage.

IV

Fifty-two Definite Articles

for Kenneth Koch

the footfall

exactly what you want to start
this poem, something altogether
Pindaric, a literal foot falling
as this first poetic foot falls
or an emblematic foot, a foot
cut and galled, inevitably turned
toward sacrifice, jackboot or wingtip,
leather heels striking along
a concrete corridor, sharp echoings
or a running shoe's thwawk
against sun-bathed asphalt
or a baby's foot slapping wet vinyl

the swan

a figure of increase or of presence,
a figure of untroubled movement

the problem of living

in Kowloon she said,
"wind is as certain as stone,"
in Gaeta, "love may be sudden
or gradual; most things
vary by predictable degrees,
but passion always seems more
than you would have imagined"

the upright piano

in an Oriental darkness, birdsongs;
long hair is lifted across lamplight,
then falls; fingers busy at braidwork;
how many years? O sages, how many?

the saxophone solo

she hummed along so softly
it seemed more breath than music;
that was in Axum where we found
her profile etched in stone

the Whitmanesque dooryard

each Spring this lilac shakes out
its heart-shaped leaves and blossoms,
and I think every time of waterbirds
and western stars and Walt Whitman,
then of Lincoln, I suppose, but only
as an afterthought, an accident
of flower and poem, curious in its
lack of eventual consequence

the drift of occasions

wavefoam or waveform and what eddies
from this oartip slips away into
our ship's own frothy past; seaways
are strange both here and in China;
water and wave mechanics, their random
certainties make some Homeric moments,
some So-shu more or less inevitable

the symbolic gesture

as ever romantic, as waves
in their crashing, as clouds

and their shadows, as hayricks
and wagons, as Constable's vision,
as sun-drenched and supple, as much
as you wanted, as sweet as can be

the sounds of the harbor

a matter of surfeit
or a surfeit of matter,
a figure, then, of fullness,
so things billow toward us
like sails full of seasounds,
that's how Arthur Dove put it

the primitive system

between darkness and keyboard,
between wavefall and shore,
between here and that treeline

the exquisite mandrill

"is it a love poem? did he sing of war?
is it an intrigue?" sing, sing, she said
a drew a quill along taut strings

the space in an angle

marked by denial, as though
these intervals between sounds
were sounds and this span
of bare canvas was space

the fisherman caught in his nets
the wavering bodies

river grasses, characters set down
near sleep, phoenix and falcon;
I have dreamed these flickerings, tongues
she fashions into songs among water

the thirty or so tables

"it's been a long time, hasn't it,"
she says, disguised as Lauren Bacall

the skin, white as snow

"O Nicholai Nicholaiovitch,"
she cried, "nightclouds and camphor"

the minister's fingers
the 6th of July

    Katchaturian played by Gilels, summer
heaving; it was a time when music seemed
precise in its sympathetic magic, Bach
on Sunday afternoons, Wanda Landowska,
her thin fingers among flowering shrubs
and Leinsdorf's Bartok weighted with desire;
Byzantine, your offering of an unsheathed
LP to the room, middle finger and thumb
spanning all that was delicate in sound

the ragged lawn

    seven days of maple seeds, wind flung
and delicately spinning, their veins
like veins in locusts' wings; is this
pattern a pattern of desire or need?

the green step
the chartreuse plain

    "think of it as a test, Sir Knight,
cart and sword bridge, bare bitter

places where everything is in doubt;
put your trust in memory and desire,"
she said, her face cowled in shadows

the lamplight
the Pleides

if time is measured by what is lost
and loss is understood in time,
sorrow is another name for order;
that seems a bit oversure of itself;
look at it this way, time passes,
the constellations come and go;
early and late, they are signs
of both change and recurrence;
alone can be either temporary or
permanent; it all depends on you

the Oregon Trail

a hundred-and-two in the shade
and precious little of that;
west of Grand Island, her hand
momentarily cool on your wrist

the ample white roadway
the binomial theorem

> both are figures of plenty,
> but if a stone winks back at you
> or 'plus or minus' occurs just like
> a prefix, this is an instance of France

the description of rivers

> myself with mine own eye I saw
> most clearly, but when I looked
> with God's eye, only God I saw;
> now I can see a river clear enough,
> its bordered water, only a river segment;
> as river, though, I see what I reflect:
> sky and clouds and a fringe of trees;
> when I see myself leaning into a river,
> I am rippled to pieces among bright things

the once Roaring Tinker

> among these several melodies,
> she thinks or I think she thought,
> is something of an earlier laughter,

a simple configuration of delight,
like punchwork outlines in a metal lamp,
bright, sudden, rudimentary and strange

the frail line of sight

early in their movement, as a sign
of solidarity, she became a surveyor,
and if anything, his passion increased
watching her, outside Wichita, her eye
glued to her transept, her arms waving

the newspaper's "death car"
the half-read novella

now lamplight seems inadequate,
its story painfully familiar,
so much desire and then confusion;
traveling northward by train from Odessa,
page after page of small-talk and stubble

the certain constriction
the mode of causal efficacy

I will explain: a body which is large
when seen near, appears small at a distance;

we are all scientists, measuring things
against things; blink one eye, then the other
quickly, and watch the Leaning Tower jump

the potted plant

a figure of surcease

the freshly sized canvas

so I says to him, Clyfford, I says,
these colors are certainly vivid,
but is life, in your view, this jagged?

the vibrating weed stalk

a figure of value in a universe of chance

the new coat of varnish
the structural grammar

toward Taormina, then,
as might have held sway,
blue sea behind us,
O bright Apollo!

the sprigs of Scotch heather
the half-muttered comment

    Christina Georgina, your name itself
    makes our century seem about to end

the advent observer
the lurking suspicion

    "if" proposes "then," "this" "that";
    your misgivings are, I might say,
    expected; think of it as Toby Tyler
    run off to join the circus but joining,
    instead, a three-ring course in linguistics;
    Ludwig is under his desk again
    and 20th century thought is wadded like gum
    above his head, pink and green and gray

the blue cast of shadows

    and if it rains, a close star at four,
    a damp autograph; you'll say it's for your sister
    and run like mad along the running board

the aging proponent

    when Lysias spoke, Athenians listened;
    it might have been his well-formed sentences
    or sunlight in his hair, his godly stance
    or practiced gesturing; ah Lysias, they'd say,
    better, by far, than that upstart Plato

the No. 2 pencil

    "resolution," she says, "matters more
    than mere purpose; anyone can want;
    would-be lovers are a dime-a-dozen;
    life is full of success stories, agile
    young dancers, singers pale with song;
    what you need is a sense that if you fail
    the world will fail with you, that calm
    villages, peaceful country scenes, lake
    districts shimmering at sunset, cities
    in their noontime gaiety will tremble
    and fall and with them, alas, via sacras,
    their stately paving stones worn smooth
    with devotion, mountain valleys, heavenly

piazzas, heavy midwestern American elms,
Athens and its wooden walls, all you have
preserved in your devotion to beauty"

the "altar of heaven"

in some places faith makes perfect sense;
that Michelangelo seems to have visited
so many of them before you and left
his mark seems quite reasonable, as well

the great bearded iris

it is, as always, a question
of metaphysics; nobody knows,
or perhaps merely a matter
of language, a tendency in words
towards what we might call entities;
you mean to say, it's just words
after all, centuries of fret, great
minds agaggle, all that troubled
reasoning, torment and sacrifice?

the pinpoint of light

in afternoon sunlight Dutch irises glow
their own saturated purples, and yellow
tongues of pollen clamor for bees

the face in that window

or merely, perhaps, a blank space,
something to hanker after, a smudge
that seems to stare back at us,
a black hole, so much of nothing that
it keeps everything it has to itself

the desolate chimera

a figure of separation, bright phosphors,
hand two waves from fingers, smile parted
by troughs and troughs of darkness, archaic
torso quavering its message by fathoms

the smiling hotel door

a figure of acceptance in a whirling dance

the absolute stanza

has a rhyme that's so perfect
(you guessed it was coming!)
that sense seems to stall there,
like a balsa-wood glider
or your lover, whose dreams pause,
as you lie down beside her;
then flight takes its new arc,
and her breath is a weather
and you soar like a bi-plane
through its sentence together

Notes

"A Place That's Known":

> "I'd like to leave it all behind . . ." and the title, from "Let the Rest of the World Go By" (Ernest Ball and Keirn Brennan, 1919), a popular song during WWI. Kearney, site of the Nebraska State Tubercular Sanitarium.

"Somewhat Gray and Graceful":

> Title and initial image from a photograph by Manuel Alvarez-Bravo.

"From the Petrarchan Folio":

> The folio in the poem is *Petrarca Canzoniere*, Northern Italy (probably Milan), late 14th century, at The Pierpont Morgan Library, described in Michael Jasenas, *Petrarch in America* (1974).

"As Semblance, Though":

> Epigraph, from Eugenio Montale, *Ossi di Sepia* (1928) "Codesto solo oggi possiamo dirti, ciò che *non* siamo, ciò che *non* vogliamo."

(This is the only thing that we can tell you today, that which we are *not*, that which we do *not* want.)

"And This Is Free":
 "this film," *And This Is Free*, a documentary film by Mike Shea about Maxwell Street blues music.

"Sequence Composed on Gray Paper":
 "glass bottle," David Mahler's composition, "Rising Ground," is based in part on the sounds made by spinning objects.

"Incidental Music":
 "what he said, what she said," from A.K. Ramanujan's translation of ancient Tamil love poetry, *Interior Landscapes* (Indiana, 1967).

"As Ever":
 Epigraph, from the title of Cartesian dialogue, *La recherche de la vérité par la lumière naturelle*.

"52 Definite Articles":
 "Ludwig is under the desk again," from a Norman Malcom Wittgenstein anecdote; the chewing gum is, however, hypothetical.

COLOPHON

The text was set in Garamond, a typeface originally designed by Claude Garamond (1500–61) in Paris in the 1530s. His style was modeled after the De Aetna roman by Adlus Manutius in 1455. This century has seen many reworked versions of Garamond from such famous designers as Frederic Goudy, M.F. Benson, and T.M. Cleland. The typeface was popular in the sixteenth through the eighteenth century used by Francois I of France and Christopher Plantin in Antwerp.

Composed by Alabama Book Composition, Deatsville, Alabama. The book was printed by Data Reproductions Corporation, on acid-free paper.

This first edition is limited to one thousand copies
of which the first twenty-seven are lettered.

———